ABOUT THE AUTHOR

Yasmina Nuny is a poet from Guinea-Bissau. She was born in Portugal and raised in different African countries before moving to the UK for her studies.

She began performing in 2016 at open mic events around Birmingham and owes a lot to the second city for her development as an artist. She has since been featured at events like Heaux Noire (London), Funkenteleky (Birmingham) and the Verve Poetry Festival R.A.P. Party (Birmingham).

Yasmina has also had her poetry published in two other Verve collections, including The Poetry Jam Anthology *Wild Dreams & Louder Voices* (2018) and Nafeesa Hamid's *Besharam* (2018).

Twitter: @yasmeeener
Facebook: https://www.facebook.com/yasminanuny

Yasmina Nuny
Anos Ku Ta Manda

VERVE
POETRY PRESS
BIRMINGHAM

PUBLISHED BY VERVE POETRY PRESS
Birmingham, West Midlands, UK
www.vervepoetrypress.com
mail@vervepoetrypress.com

All rights reserved
© 2019 Yasmina Nuny

The right of Yasmina Nuny to be identified as author of this work has been asserted in accordance with section 77 of the Copyright, Designs and Patents Act 1988.

No part of this work may be reproduced, stored or transmitted in any form or by any means, graphic, electronic, recorded or mechanical, without the prior written permission of the publisher.

FIRST PUBLISHED MAR 2019

Printed and bound in the UK
by Imprint Digital, Exeter

ISBN: 978-1-912565-19-1

Cover Image Design by Patricia Bandora

Garandi k jungutu
Ta ma oja lunju
di ke mininu k sikidu.

Noh kontinua bata garandi son.

CONTENTS

Part One - Ami

Haikus	10
Gazing	11
Directions for a journey home	12
Bissau bedju	13
Self	14
Nha retaguarda	15
Bariga	15
Bissau Daily	16

Part Two - Kerensa

Haikus	18
The voicemail I would include in my mixtape of only ballads	19
Staying soft	20
Transatlantic love	21
Lessons on love as explored by the cast of the best television series out there	23

Grey	24
Underneath guiding lights and hidden from cold places	25
Tongue twister	26
Imagine love	28

Part Three - Libri

Haikus	31
Free	32
Best consumed by	33
A BLACK woman walks into a church	34
Expletives	38
Audre taught me	39
When Kanye ain't read the footnotes – After Jasmine Mans	41
A word to the Black Girls	46

Introducing Darnell Thompson-Gooden and Ayọ

Glossary and acknowledgements

Anos Ku Ta Manda

Ami

I

Graffiti is the
best student DIY when
schools do not function.

II

You called it state of
siege. Now that you can see them,
please pay attention.

III

Bissau is burning.
The presidential palace
is quite unbothered.

IV

Deus kuma "bô bim,
n mostra bos kaminhu
di vitória."

Gazing

There is something romantic about homes I am never in long
    enough to demystify.
I place bent and burnt buildings in poetic pictures, construct them
    for consumption,
for foreign and half-foreign gazes, like mine,
it is almost imperial.

So, I deconstruct the romance; pull fibre from fibre to find
    inconsistency
and instead notice that the black star emblem cannot pull away
    from my skin.
The familiarity of home will not allow it.
Light is consistent so long as you have a candle handy.
I read my Kriol by it.
My custom by it.
My politics by it and the romance dims.

Enlightenment will do that,
as will the tyres burning in the capital,
and I know that in remaining, or returning,
Guinean has always been.

Directions for a journey home

I know of transience; lived it.
Short periods at a time.
Contexts of now only threaded by expectations of what's to come;
But they are fragments, nonetheless.

For now, I exist here.
Older, hopefully wiser.
That is to say that I am not likely to get lost and/or forget my way
        back to
roots, when it is only a prayer away,
only a generation ahead.
Only God and mother, and the Amen at the end of these
        journeys,
and years, and   separations,
and oceans, and borders/and lonely mornings, and
goodbyes.

Nostalgia is bittersweet. But we move.
We write of the movement; joining the fragments through
        sentences, separating with comas, enjambments and
semi-colons instead of full stops until God,
the final Amen,
Amen.

Bissau bedju

Bissau ku nha pape kunsi na si mininessa ka parsi ku Bissau
    di ahos.
Cidadi na garandi, ma i na luta ku si bedjussa.
Prassa intchi ku lembranssa di imperialismu,
Storias k no rekonkista pa futuro Guineense.
Soh monumento di esforço da raça k sikidu tchan na Império,
i na lembra di tempus k si dunus mora ba na ki palacio k
    sta inda la.
I ka sibi kuma kolon bai si kaminhu. No cerca elis disna.
I ka sibi kuma na e tchon li,
anos ku ta manda.

Self

An apology to;
a memory of;
a reimagination.
Radical representation,
taking up all the

s p a c e.

Expanding into comfort, into home.

Did you know how far
skin could
stretch?
Have you seen the marks on my body from it?

My tongue is full and
quick
to make me swell with pride
every time I refuse to swallow it back
for you.

Every time I refuse to do the work
for
you.

Nha retaguarda

Eh ka negan nha garandessa.
Ma... tudo garandi k n'na garandi,
N ka mati badjudessa di nha mame.

    Eh stan dianti, lisons di vida na elis k n ta djubil.
    Eh stan tras,
    nha suguranssa.

Bariga

    N'na massa mon di nha mame ku mentolatu,
    nha dona sikidu pertu mi.

Bissau Daily

"Entidadis religiosas
bo djuda pa kaba ki grevi
na escolas publicas."

"Bo paga no pursoris,
no misti bai escola."

Didn't you know that, everywhere,
students are the ones who begin the
revolution?
And here at Império, right on your doorstep, is where Bissau
turns
phoenix
from the ashes of your
mandate.

Kerensa

I

Reminders you've left
on my thighs of the safety
of your steady arms.

II

I'm not much of a
talker. But for you I'll learn
to soliloquize.

III

I can be a peace,
and also of shit, but you
bring out the former.

IV

Let's go on dates and
talk about dismantling
love's power structures

The voicemail I would include in my mixtape of only ballads

All this to say that separation stretches
long and
far and
hearts are fonder and,
maybe running away don't make sense
and all we have left to express the longing
is nausea,
dirty looks and
butterflies.

Staying soft

Thank God for sponge hearts
that absorb joy
and scrub the slate clean of pain
for openness to
love.

A requiem for un-love.
A letter to re-love.

To be loved
and love (back) fiercely,
is surely of
God.

Prayers for love returned,
and Amen.

Transatlantic love

We've got that transatlantic crossing
type love.
I mean, you crossed my path and I welcomed you back to
    tha muthaland
type love.
That sô abô k n cre,
mi nuh wa nuh-body else
type love.

Forgive my accent,
but we can combine my kriol to your patois and speak in
    languages that only
you and I can understand.

Cause, baby, we got the reggae and gumbe type slow jams playing
    between our
bodies
to   di   riddim of   our   combined   heart/beats
until the morning.

Our minds, whining with each other until bodiless forms are
    just one
and I don't want nobody else grabbing on my waist and
tasting the French on my lips quand tu me tiens au chaud la
    nuit entire.
Baby, it's just you and me on the dance floor tonight.

And when tomorrow comes, you're still dancing around my mind,
slowly moving with my emotions until you're stuck on repeat.
Stuck
on –
stuck –
and repeat.
I hope that I got you hooked on my melody.
Kriol and patois sewed into this poetry makes for beautiful music.

My slams keep turning into slow jams around you.
You got me singing these words back to you in tongues I never
spoke before.
Baby, I'm remixing my Guiné with your JA. May your soul keep
      jammin' with mine on a dance floor of their own design
         through the night.
And I hope they be
                stuck
on each other. Like a beautifully scr-scr-atched vinyl
turned classic. Turned legacy.
And we won't ever get tired of this.

Cause this right here, this Afro/West Indian heart drumbeat, don't
      ever go out of style so long as you and I
keep it grooving.

Lessons on love as explored by the cast of the best television series out there

1. If you have chemistry, you only need one other thing: timing. But timing's a bitch.
2. If you want to keep someone around, you do something about it.
3. Love doesn't make sense. You can't logic your way in or out of it... Love is the best thing we do.

I've traced all the little reasons for the big things in my life – for you in my life. Now I want to tell the whole world about the story of how I met you because it has, thus far, been

lengen-wait-for-it-

dary.

Legendary.

True story

Grey

I don't often appreciate greyness.
I don't ever appreciate rain.
Existing in this place has often felt like
flooding,
drowning in nostalgia for home.

But grey begets green; I learned that in the mist
at the gates of heaven,
where rain washed me and my love new again and
where we could sprout and bloom again.
I wrapped my tendrils around his trunk and branches and waited
      for elevation skywards,
sunwards.

Underneath guiding lights and hidden from cold places

It always smell like a home-cooked meal when I come round. That is all the assurance I need outside of words that the stars promised you to me for a while; as long a while as you gon have me and watch me grow like the love we sat under on that cold day, sheltering us from the wind and snow.

I been savoring on that feeling ever since.

I'm not sure too many people feel like home when I am miles away from what I knew, but you the closest thing I have to it. And you make it feel like the type home with a skylight, where we can be dancing underneath the same stars that brought you to me. My north light, you always pointing me in the right direction, and I guess that's why I don't ever feel too lost, except in you. And I'm hoping that it's somewhere tucked in your heart, in a safe place, underneath guiding lights and hidden from cold places where my love go numb.

A place where it always smell like you and your home-cooked meals.

Tongue twister

Touch your tongue to my toes and drag them to the nook of my knees,
'til you taste the wet teasing my thighs.
Then dip the tip of your pinky in the tightness of my p—.
Taint my neck with teeth and I'll tear through your torso.

Tickle my arched spine till I turn toward you like say
take me.
And you do,
hands tentative on my tummy,
then tucked underneath trembling t—.

Twist your tongue against mine;
touch my heart something fierce with tokens of you.
Tell me truths that only I will know at these sun-timid times,
when we stoke fires and tease them into a slow burn like,
baby take your time tonight.

Talk to me in the in-betweens.
We can knot futures in kisses and tangle our tongues in promises.
Tie our tomorrows in these moments, in our todays,
make them stretch until we're moaning,
until it's morning,
until we're tired but more alive than ever.

And then do it all over again three times fast.
And then slow.
And then fast again,
until we find our rhythm.
Until we reach our peaks.

And then do it again in your mother tongue.
And then again until I match it
with my own.

And then again until it sounds carnal.
Until it sounds like a prayer.
Oh God. Yes.
Amen.

Until it's just breathing each other in,
tied up and transformed and thankful for tonight,
for tomorrow,
and for this.

Imagine love

Tomorrow we would have sat on our front porch again. The one that my darling and I built up from the ground in the earthy colors that remind us that anything can grow in the right conditions. And we managed to. Grow, that is. Old, in faith, in love, and tomorrow would have ripened us, and our children. I pray that they see tomorrow. And we would have sat there, watching the wind and listening to each other as we always have, and I will be reminded of those short moments that have led to this lifetime and I would have thanked God, again, again.

On some days, I would be worried that our children wouldn't get the chance to develop the wisdom lines that form by the corner of my darling's eyes whenever I got him chuckling, and my own get dewy when I start worrying like this. But my darling, he told me that we raised them vulnerable enough to let God transform and strengthen them and my heart settles again. I think that's why I chose to love him; he always makes my faith feel new and child-like again, even after I've lost count of the days that we've sat under this sun, letting it feed us into our majesty.

People forget it sometimes, that we are human. That we hurt when we lose a brother, that we revolt when enough is enough. They forget our joy too. Or resent it. But I stopped settling for apologism a long time ago. I was taught that it was redundant, and that is what I try to teach all the children that step onto my porch. How would I have built it up, my peace of mind, if I had kept apologizing for it? And from the day I started minding my own shea and coconut oil, man have I grown stronger. Healthier.

Fierce, because I have refused to let this learned shame be my unbecoming.

And I like sitting here with my darling thinking about what we've been through together, and I feel proud when I look out to the sunflower fields we tended to for decades. Where my baby girls and boys ran through as toddlers. I get overwhelmed with nostalgia sometimes when we reminisce about those youthful nights. Me, loud and revolutionary. Him, pensive. And also revolutionary. Those nights where we laughed and made love and spoke about the supernatural until I inevitably fell asleep on his heart. And my own heart is warmed, like the yellow of the sunflowers and the honeyed milk that smooths his voice when I think that he has kept me in his heart for all these years.

And today as we sit here, I thank God for the blessings and the moments and this lifetime. And I thank God for my darling, and for my children. And I thank God for me and for today.

Again, again.

> \- *For the love that will come unexpectedly.*
> *For the one who will stay.*

Libri

I

The glossary is
political. As are the
missing translations.

                                    II

                     Black power's not real.
                     Only magic can explain
                            negro excellence.

III

I guess I don't know
if I'm a freedom fighter
or just ungrateful.

                                    IV

                            Propaganda is
                     my favorite part of the
                       making of this book.

Free

I have loved myself to this
place.
To this state.
Enough to preserve when needed,
cry when needed,
war when needed.
Shave, regrow, rebirth
as needed.
Bloom where it is possible,
learn from all of it.
Unlearn to apologize for it –
for
myself.
We been there already,
done that already.
No longer at peace with disrespecting
God
like that.

Best consumed by

Baby, you smell like some rich cocoa butter,
round cheeks sweet chocolate face.
Looking like a snack baby.
Come here and let me get a
taste.
Bring that pretty ass next to me,
let me grab hold of your waist.
Show me what those hips do
While I secure you by your braids.
I'll whisper in your ear,
lick all my cravings away.

I've run through all possible scenarios. His fellas laugh it off, but
    the reality is hella scary though.
But I'm tripping and he's pimping, and they're missing the whole
    point.
I know that this brother and his brothers don't hold themselves
    accountable.

A **BLACK** woman walks into a church

When they tell you that your **BLACK** pride is the same as white
        nationalism, they will frame it Biblically.
They will say that Jesus should be the center of our identity, as if
        this skin wasn't Scriptured and crafted out of the very
        same dark ink that wrote the Bible through and through.
They will tell you that **BLACK** pride is the reason for division.
As if **BLACK** pride wasn't the remedy born out of all this
        self-hatred, and I know it's easy...
It's easy to reject identity politics when
default
makes you person before color.
It's easy to reject identity politics when you forget that
Jesus' hair was as nappy as mine is.

When they tell you about your **BLACK** pride, they will use the
        word boast.
They will say it right after praise and worship,
right after you have already given thanks to your God
for loving all that you are underneath all of that
#melaninonfleek or #blackgirlmagic.
And you will
sit there,
wondering if you've been worshipping the wrong God when you
        stepped past the threshold
of this here church.

When they talk about how loud your **BLACKNESS** is, they will
 giggle nervously as if they are half joking.
They will tell you to hear them out and you will feel yourself
 shrink in your seat,
back into invisibility. They had
the caucasity to snatch your platform again,
just so that they could highlight their sensitivities about how **BLACK BLACK PANTHER** was.
As if I haven't counted the cinematic minutes that I've been forced
to relate to characters that never looked
like me.
The directors never looked
like me.
God, tell me why they don't like me.

They don't like my joy.
They cannot allow this joy, but they will say it is not their intention.
They like to talk about
intention.

But what good is intention when I've started using their whitewash
 as bleach to scrub off all this too BLACK?
So, excuse me, but your intentions are for all intents and purposes
 cancelled from now on.
They will be
handled
from now on.
These hands are not afraid to leave their dark marks on white
 supremacy anymore.

When they tell you how loud your **BLACKNESS** is, make it
bold and CAPS the fuck out of your **PRIDE**.
~~Cut them off by~~ SPEAKING EVEN LOUDER.

Make sure that the motherfuckers at the back hear this shit.
I won't
repeat
this shit
'Cause I'm fucking tired of being made to feel like this.
Being made to kneel at his white ego.

When they tell you to make Jesus the center, tell them the Lord
made you **BLACK** for a reason.
Tell them that you birthed the
whole
of fucking humanity.
That sounds pretty damn Biblical to me.
Why shouldn't I be proud of what the Lord made me?
I was *fearfully and wonderfully made*, and don't you ever forget it.

If they ever try that shit again, you know...
Talking
about your **BLACK** skin, show them the names inked on it.
It will be the only time that you will do this, and then tell them that
      they are not names you pulled out of sensationalized
      news articles.
Tell them it's your brother,
your light-skinned and dark-skinned sisters, your lover.
It's you
getting your nappy hair checked at the airport for drugs.
It's you
being held in cells for days for walking while **BLACK**.

It's you
being ridiculed in classrooms,
being gasped at, at the ATM like you don't have a bank account to
    withdraw from.
You must surely want to fucking rob them

    It's you that they keep silencing
    even at the pulpit of your own church.
They will squeeze at your throat until you speak of your pain no
    more because
white supremacy likes to play
god.
That sure the fuck will not be the center of this here **BLACK** as fuck
    identity.

And if they ever have anything else to say about this loud and
    boastful **BLACKNESS** let it be nothing more
than *Hallelujah* and
Amen.

                                                   - *Psalm 139:14*

Expletives

I've been told in the past that I got a foul mouth.
Been told it's not lady-like, and I find that pretty
fucking funny
'cause everyone and their mama curses.
And I'm a
grown ass woman.
I've no interest in being a lady when it gets to be so inconvenient.
Imagine not having the freedom to tell people to
fuck off
when they tell me to be a lady. Can't be me.

I been told I don't need to curse to get my point across.
That my poetry is powerful enough without it. But
shit, there is something remarkable about how
intentionally
I do it.
So I think that my message comes across
pretty fucking clear.
And it is
pretty damn crystal from this poem how little a
fuck
I give about offence being taken from the way I share
my fucking opinions.
So thank you for yours, but
I am doing fucking alright as is.

Audre taught me

I told them I was tired of the conversation.
Invalidation seems second nature, as if entitlement to pussy gave
    them a second set of lips.
As if pussy was performed.
As if they even could.
As if they didn't feed into the patriarchy with this privilege; as if I
    didn't do the same with all these internalizations.
As if patriarchy was a conscious decision that we made or
    unmade every day.
As if I wouldn't have dismantled it whole by now if it was.
As if men, genuinely, wanted it
dismantled.

This conversation hurts.
My mama asked me why, I told her it's because loving men is a
    toxic habit that I picked up somewhere along the way.
They told me be grateful, you don't know the suffering
    of the past.
As if sisters have not been mourned daily since.
Here we still are, experiences mansplained as if they were not
    ours.
As if black womanhood didn't belong to me.

Then again,
maybe it doesn't.
So, I get tired of owing and owing for a body I cannot own.
Boycott for preservation.

Men been raised on broken mirrors and entitlement. And me?
They say I been raised wrong. This poem is just
rambling irrationally about false realities.
Reaching for reasons to radicalize.
Ranting.
Hormonal again. Ridiculous to them.
Men are self-important. They think I'm self-righteous.
Boycott as social commentary.

Men act like they don't have work to do. Like,
Let the women do the work
for you.
They don't care for the truth, it distracts from the throne they
    sit on.
Truth is an inconvenience to self-importance. That's why they
    like to talk
for me.

Boycott because they don't know they need me.
They're self-important.
They don't know that entitlement never taught them to be
self-sufficient.

When Kanye ain't read the footnotes – After Jasmine Mans

This can't be what it looked like when God sent his only son
    down from heaven to meet us.
Trading verses for 280 characters,
spitting false knowledge to disrespect ancestors,
dropping out of college don't seem to have done you justice.
Now all these false prophets ain't down to join the protests, he
    said he don't want to get his
Yeezys dirty.

Who you gonna call now that you've fallen down so far from Grace?
Negro it's gonna take a lot more than three or four baptisms to get
    you saved on the land where niggas like you
praise white Jesus, name them Massa then
blame the slaves.
Like say, they ain't suffered to get you to this place.
Like say, they ain't been talking to God every single damn day.
Negro they ain't sending they smiles down your way nomore.

Ye you forgot who you was before.

You forgot how you and Emmett Till could have been brothers.
You forgot that black lives are sacrificed for white lies in places
    like Mississippi.
That Calabasas accent ain't fooling nobody.
Ye you forgot that you was part of the people in Chi valley.
Even Jesus ain't burn crosses on the lawns of his enemies.
Negro we weren't supposed to be enemies.

But I guess you started dressing just like them. Moved in
then started speaking just like them.
Got in the Sam's club alright, just like them.
Brother you forgot that you were always scum to them, a
nigger in their eyes.

What?
You thought that when money got you out the southside you
                could act like racism wasn't still alive?
Like money and marriage was gonna make you white?
Right?

Nigga ain't no such thing as a
white nigger.

Ye it was better when they got you quiet.
They called a war on black bodies and you called it
suicide.

It's funny how when old Ye's words came alive,
flashing lights, and chalk outlines,
streets erupting in protest cries,
you closed your eyes and asked the world to open they minds
like:

it don't exist if i don't see that shit.
Like, how is it all of y'all that's slaves to this?
I just want to think free and move past the hate you give.
Ye you forgot it's they that's been hating us...
Strange fruit don't taste quite
    as sweet as when
        it's
        still
        hang-
        ing fro-
        m a
              tree.
Can't have too many   niggers
running around thinking that they're   free.
'Cause then they just might start thinking that they too have the
    right to
speak.
So leave just enough room to breathe and
let Kanye do the preaching.
Ye, you played this charade for too long and started thinking that
    you was the messiah.
In the process, you forgot all the reasons why we riot.
How they hold guns to us and fire,
then leave the rest to cry in Bibles.
Call out to God, but just get
your replies.

Negro I'm tired of your twitter fingers
justifying all these trigger fingers,
then denying all these racial systems, and say you're
trying to uplift us it's just we

gotta liberate our minds and stop milking all this
 victimhood,
as if little black children weren't growing up in ghetto
 neighborhoods singing:

Jesus walk.
Jesus walk with me.
Can you hear them singing?
Jesus walk
God show me the way because the devil's trynna break me down.
Jesus walk with me.

Ain't that what you proclaimed yourself to be?
Well nigga you was just blasphemy.
I wanna believe that love is your philosophy,
but it's dangerous to dismiss your ancestry like your mama ain't
 been at the sit-ins
for a reason. Ye,
you pulled up a seat at the white counter and forgot we was
 protesting.
Forgot we was still at war with racism,
as if regular black folk ain't got the cops called on them just
 for existing...

But nigga we living.
The best way we know how given the circumstances.
We're not withholding love, you're just tripping.
 Black People I Love You,
  signed, Alicia Garza.
It's a movement,
love's the movement.
But what your words are telling me is that black people
are the least deserving.

We're not trynna silence you but brother we're hurting, and
Jesus is still weeping, burdened.
Our ancestors are rising on the other side, determined.
We are the Israelites, here to claim our rights. Even
Yeezus
can't stand in the way of the promised life.

A word to the Black Girls

My first pick is my afro pick with a pro Black fist for this nappy thick, and my ass thick too...

Yeah, i look real cool with my natural aesthetic but profit less than cosmetic
when the capitalists rule.

Yeah, the highlight's inherent, but let's not pretend that you like it better when
Black girls do it first.
'Cause you been laughing at my skin, while filling vials with melanin.
For how much they be selling it?
Like i ain't do all the work.

I know my worth.

Don't feel the verse then throw out the words cause this truth is hurt.
But also, impossibly nuanced.
I read scripture,
paint and,
t-tuh-twerk,
all while teaching little Black girls how to navigate this world that
don't seem to ever want 'em.

Like how my mama teach me to be a Black woman like how her mama learned how to become one.
Powerful enough even to threaten systems and isms that need us broken.

We've spoken. Over and over and
over
again.
Of the struggle we're born in

But this Black girl blues ain't stolen our joy we've proven it.
Mostly to ourselves, (and whoever else is listening).
But we told 'em.

This Black girl magic saucy,
drip-dripping,
and ain't that something?

This existence, winning at every intersection. Mother Maya said it,
      we're rising.

How many times you say Black girl in conversation?
My body language hella repetitive with it (Black girl).
Poetic with it (Black girl).
Step into the room and be yelling with it (Black girl).
It's lit (Black girl).
Like make sure you're acknowledging this Black girl.
Can't be getting sick of us Black girls.
Not when you profit from us Black girls.
Listen to
the Black girls.

We ain't voiceless just unmute us a bit.
We're louder than you ever would have imagined it. Imagine this:
Gravity is like a myth to us. We're elevated, our God is lifting us.
Pretending we're not there is getting dangerous cause we'll leave
      silently and take the magic with us,
and then what?

What's a body without a spine?
What's left of you when it was always all mine?

You can scar my body fifty-four different times,
displace me from mama house and I'll still find my tribe.
Keep in mind a whole village took part in raising me like *that's my
    daughter too.*

This love story among Black women is truly the most beautiful.
Don't @ me like you got a clue of what we're surviving through.
Of what we have done for
you.
We don't forget the measures we've taken to
hold on to mama Africa's native tongue and truth.

Can't never stray too far from these roots
when teaching these fruits
how to handle the bruises that they're living through.
The same lessons life taught us too.

But enjoy it Black girl you're wonderful and they won't ever be
    through hunting you,
but your God ain't done loving you.
I will be loving you,
like how my mama keep loving me too,
keep loving me through,
so, keep loving your truth.

It's a word.

Introducing

I would like to introduce two poets whose visions and voices:
1. have so gracefully complemented my own and,
2. are deserving of standing alone and being celebrated as such.

Thank you for your honesty.
Thank you for your power.

Darnell Thompson-Gooden
Darnell is a young spoken word poet born and raised in a Nottingham, of Jamaican heritage. He began writing poetry in his early teens and has since used it as a creative avenue to express personal feelings, thoughts and experiences, often exploring themes such as romance, personal empowerment, appreciation for his family and more. A music enthusiast, Darnell often draws inspiration from a variety of music genres for his poetry and occasionally incorporates singing into his spoken word pieces. He can be found on Instagram under @dizzy_tg

Ayọ̀
Ayọ̀ is a London-based, Nigerian-born poet and writer exploring the facets of being Black British and an immigrant. When she is not writing, she is working towards an MBChB in Medicine. Her short poems can be found on Instagram under @ayowrites.

Poems about her
Darnell

I write poems about her...
I write poems about her to help myself get over the break up.
To remind myself of the reasons why at that time I thought it was
        time to break up.
I write poems about her as a reminder that something beautiful can
        still come out of an ugly situation.
That even though they say actions speak louder than words, the
        power held in semantics is still enough to hurt a soul.
I'm not talking sticks and stones,
it took me too long to realise just how much words meant to her.
I write poems about her to remind myself of all that I've learnt in the
        process of leaving her.
And yes, it makes me quite sad that I no longer have faith that it will
        be her that I apply it to but that's just the way life goes.

I write poems about her because I will not let go of who she is.
Because she still is.
Still continues to be important to me.
A phenomenal being,
she continues to live phenomenally.
Phenomenal woman.
Once considered to be a missing piece,
she has still contributed to the puzzle as I am forming the current
        incomplete image of me.
All that she has added is invaluable.

I write poems about her to help myself get through the 5 stages
    of grief.
I'd be lying if I denied the fact that sometimes I was selfish,
and If I said it didn't hurt me when she got angry and gave the cold
    shoulder.
I'd have rather we talked it out,
tried to bargain and come to an agreement about what I could change
    to make her feel better.
The sadness that followed was so intense that I can't imagine what it
    must be like to handle depression.
7 months later, after a lot of self-reflection and putting pen to paper,
    I'm arriving upon the stage of acceptance.
Accepting that most times we have options.
We must live by the decisions we make, regardless of whether the
    consequences may be hard to face,
we must learn to accept them.

I write poems about her to remember the good times we had.
Like the first date when we went for Jamaican food and afterwards she
    bought me ice cream.
It's funny 'cause at the time I didn't think it was a date, though she did.
But in retrospect it definitely was our first date.
I recall on the train ride we spoke about religion and sexuality
At that time, I was a virgin.
Not just sexually
But also in my capacity to show appreciation regularly.
She changed both things for me.

I write poems about her to remind myself that even though we're no longer together, I can still appreciate her and our memories.
Those cold mornings spent between the sheets.
her room often smelt like coconut oil and hot "tikka" masala tea,
so now if I smell anything similar, I am triggered.
I am reminded of the way she would look at me.
The way she would smile at me.
The way she would say my name.
The way she would say "it's okay".
The way she would laugh at my jokes even when they weren't funny.
The way she would laugh at me when I acted stupid.
The way she would comfort me when I was going through shit.
The way –
The way she would get heated when she got triggered.
The way she would talk about politics and even though it wasn't my strong suit, I would still listen.
Though I didn't always understand, I still cared.
The way she would hold me and stroke my beard.
The way she nourished my soul as well as my body with home cooked food that sometimes we enjoyed late at night,
 but for some reason always tasted better in the afternoon.

I write poems about her because I am a poet.
Most times I don't truly know how I feel until I note it down for my conscious mind to see
because my heart won't show it.
It confuses me and others too.
It's funny how someone else can stroke our ego yet it's the ones we care about most who end up getting bruised.
I write poems about her in the hope that it will help to heal her wounds
despite the fact she may never hear these words

I started writing poetry because that's what I was told the heart
        broken do.
And aside from music and the love from my loved ones
This is the only thing that helps me get through.

I write poems about her to make sense of the incoherency
And despite all the disagreements, I believe God has kept her in my
        life because she still has much to teach me.
I still appreciate all that she is,
there is still love for her.
Not romantic, but it is strong.
And the words I write are an expression of the length to which my
        reasoning can be stretched.

Mo Ti Sọ Èdè Mi Nù
Ẹ gba mi!
Ayọ̀
in Yoruba

Mo ti sọ èdè mi nù

Mo ti sùn gbàgbé
Mi o ránti ibi ti mo fi sii

Ah,
       mo ma ti sọ èdè mi nù

Mo ti jina jina, mo ti damu damu
O dabi pé mo ti ṣina

Ta lo ma rán mi lọwọ?

       Mo ti sọ èdè mi nù

Ṣe nínú ọkọ lo wa? Abi nínú ọkọ-ofurufu
ti ó gbé mi de bi?
Aṣé bí mo ṣe n júwọ si ará, ni mo ṣe n júwọ si èdè

       Mo má ti sọ èdè mi nù

Ṣe nínú àpò ọkàn lo wa? Abi nínú àlá mi lo wa?
Ṣé máa rí i lórí ahọn? Abi àtẹlẹwọ?

E jọ, tí ẹ báa ba mi rí èdè mi
Ẹ sọ fún ko padà si ile
Ẹ sọ fún ko má bínú; ọmọde lon ṣe mi
Ẹ sọ fún pé tí ó bá padà wá, èmi o ni jẹ ki ó lọ mọ

Tí ó bá dẹ fẹ sare
        bi ọmọde ṣe ń sare sínú agbami
                ẹ sọ fún pé máa sare pẹlú ẹ
                        bi ọmọde ṣe ń sare sínú ọwọ mama rẹ

Ṣùgbọn
ẹ gba mi, ẹ gba mi, ẹ gba mi

Ẹ ba mi wa èdè mi
tori aro ẹ sọ mi.

I've Lost My Tongue
Help me!
Ayọ̀
in English

 I've lost my tongue

I slept and I've forgotten
I don't remember where I've left it

Ah,
> I've lost my tongue

I've journeyed and journeyed, I've toiled and toiled
It seems I've lost my way

Who will help me?

> I've lost my tongue

Is it in the car? Or in the plane
that brought me here?
It seems as though as I was waving goodbye to my motherland,
> I was also waving goodbye to my mother tongue

> I've lost my tongue

Is it in the pockets of my heart? Or in my dreams?
Will I find it in my mouth? Or in the palm of my hands?

Please, if you come across my tongue
Tell it to come back home
Tell it not to be angry; I was childish
Tell it that if it comes back, I won't let it go again

If it wants to run
      like a child runs into the sea
            tell it I'll run with it
                  like a child runs into the arms
                      of his mother

But for now,
help me, help me, help me

Help me search for my tongue
for I miss it dearly.

GLOSSARY

Ami	Me
Anos ku ta manda	We are in charge
Badjudessa	Youth (feminine)
Bariga	Stomach/womb
Bedjussa	Old age
Cerca	Chase
Cidadi	City
Deus	God
Djuda	Help
Dona	Grandparent
Garandi	Big/Matured
Jungutu	Squat
Kaminhu	Path
Kerensa	Love
Kolon	Colonizer
Lembranssa	Memory
Libri	Free
Lissons	Lessons
Lunju	Far
Luta	Fight/Struggle
Mame	Mother
Mininessa	Childhood
Oja	To see
Pape	Father
Pursoris	Teacher (plural)
Rekonkinsta	Reconquer
Retaguarda	Rearguard
Sikidu	Standing
Suguranssa	Security
Vitoria	Victory

ACKNOWLEDGEMENTS

All praise to the Most High.

Thank you, dearest Patricia Bandora, for your beautiful cover design.
Thank you, Darnell and Ayọ for allowing me to share your words.
Thank you, Sean Colletti for your mentorship, your guidance and kindness.
Thank you to my friends, for your prayers and enthusiasm.
Thank you to my parents and siblings whose support was ever present. Mama and Papa, I apologize for some of these pieces.
Thank you Amerah Saleh and Stuart Bartholomew for believing in my work and bringing it to life.
Thank you, Bissau. Thank you, Birmingham.

ABOUT VERVE POETRY PRESS

Verve Poetry Press is a new press focussing intently on meeting a local need in Birmingham - a need for the vibrant poetry scene here in Brum to find a way to present itself to the poetry world via publication. Co-founded by Stuart Bartholomew and Amerah Saleh, with help and support from Cynthia Miller, it is publishing poets from all corners of the city - poets that represent the city's varied and energetic qualities and will communicate its many poetic stories.

Added to this is a colourful pamphlet series featuring poets who have previously performed at our sister festival - and a debut performance poetry series, which will see us working with the brightest rising stars on the UK spoken word scene.

Like the festival, we will strive to think about poetry in inclusive ways and embrace the multiplicity of approaches towards this glorious art.

www.vervepoetrypress.com
@VervePoetryPres
mail@vervepoetrypress.com